INHERITANCE

TAYLOR JOHNSON

INHERITANCE

Alice James Books
FARMINGTON, MAINE
alicejamesbooks.org

10 9 8 7 6 5 4 3 2

Alice James Books are published by Alice James Poetry Cooperative, Inc., an affiliate of the University of Maine at Farmington.

Alice James Books
114 Prescott Street
Farmington, ME 04938
www.alicejamesbooks.org

Library of Congress Cataloging-in-Publication Data

Names: Johnson, Taylor, 1991- author.
Title: Inheritance / Taylor Johnson.
Description: Farmington, ME : Alice James Books, [2020]
Identifiers: LCCN 2020016847 (print) | LCCN 2020016848 (ebook) | ISBN
9781948579131 (trade paperback) | ISBN 9781948579780 (epub)
Subjects: LCSH: Washington (D.C.)--Poetry. | LCGFT: Poetry.
Classification: LCC PS3610.O383396 I54 2020 (print) | LCC PS3610.O383396
(ebook) | DDC 811/.6--dc23
LC record available at https://lccn.loc.gov/2020016847
LC ebook record available at https://lccn.loc.gov/2020016848

Alice James Books gratefully acknowledges support from individual donors, private foundations, the University of Maine at Farmington, the National Endowment for the Arts, the Amazon Literary Partnership, and the Maine Arts Commission, an independent state agency supported by the National Endowment for the Arts.

Cover image: Deana Lawson; Trap Car, 2016; Inkjet print; 40 x 50.5 inches (101.6 x 128.3 cm); © Deana Lawson

CONTENTS

Since I quit that internet service,

A kind of wildness descends and across the expanse the attendant
wind drones its one fecund song

On Ignorance

Aubade

W 177th & Broadway

This is a review for Blue in Green by Miles Davis

Brooklyn Poem

metaphysics

Art Movie

I set out to touch it all over

My idea of abstraction is white lightning

Trans is against nostalgia

Semiotics

Lorde Blue

Conjecture on the nature of inconvenience

from the never

Chiaroscuro

Virginia Slim

The black proletarianization of the bourgeois form isn't Kanye West's gospel samples

Black existential exegesis

8th & Ingraham

June, DC

Hunger

Self-portrait in cyanotype

States of decline

Rigorous Practice of Listening

Virginia Slim

Containing Continuity
Derrida/Coleman
Similes
On my way to you

FIRST THERE WAS THE EARTH IN MY MOUTH.
HENRY DUMAS // KEF 21

SINCE I QUIT THAT INTERNET SERVICE, I'm thinking more about the transitive properties in books. The words, the palimpsest of images accruing in my brain, but more immediately the book in my hand. The cover worn at one end from sweat and gripping it when it comes close. Close as in when I stood up, let one deep exhale, when I came to the lines *Of all fearless happiness / from which reaches my life I sing—* and find it underlined by a beloved stranger. It's like turning the record over. Knowing you're hearing what I'm hearing. Easing up on the edge of the chair. It's like we're holding hands now at the edge of a white silence, from which we are to make a music of our being here, of being moved. Wherein our music compliments and holds close each other's sound. Sound in the wet room of the tree I met you in. Nothing is said about the water, or the fearless trees angled toward and against the light. Light that did fall on me, made much of me. Light that sings through me. So I'm singing.

PENNSYLVANIA AVE. SE

Bless the boys riding their bikes straight up, at midnight, touching,
if only briefly, holding, hands as they cross the light to Independence.
Bless them for from the side the one on the red bike looks like me,
his redbrown hair loose against the late summer static heat.
The boy who is not me (see how I did that) fixes his mouth to say
something I will never hear   *I love you*   or   *I'm so sad*   though
more than likely   *Catch up*. Bless the boy who is me on his bike
because he was a witness to my witnessing and did not turn away,
did not make of me a disappeared, burned thing– instead nodded as boys do.
Bless the distance and the knowing there. What my mind makes of these boys,
bless that long hallway I'm always going through.
Bless what could be mine or me.
Bless the boys I wanted to be or wanted.

NOCTURNE

What was rampant in me was not wisteria. Perhaps decay, or loss of reflection.

No one like me gets old, or so I thought, even as I watched the days fade into each other.

Was I no one? Which phrase means a grown-up girl: mica-gilded; pure myth; gone?

Thoreau might say I was trying to find the door to nothingness, that the wild was already in me.

However, I walked out my bed to find my skin, only to return moondrunk, bramble-laden,

stripped to sinew, a broken syntax. No denying how I got here, I laid down among the tall grass

and came up a specter. I came up everywhere.

LINCOLN TOWN CAR

My grandfather would spell certain words so that the dog couldn't comprehend.
Out, Food. The dog, that little bear-fighter, ran into the road one day, buried in the yard now.
And the next dog, he waited in the backroom for my grandmother to return heavy-footed from
around the corner. And when she didn't return, he remained there unreachable as language.

Something was wrong if we left the country: fluid around the heart, not enough movement,
syrup for blood. Leaving meant taking showers and my grandfather fixing my grandmother's
hair. All of us, clean-shirted, in the front seat of the Lincoln Town Car. We shared a humid
thought, pressed as we were against the maroon leather, six-legged in the front seat. Before us
the highway unraveled. Sorghum and corn and soy— collapsing as the wind fell, listening for
light. I listened for muscadines swelling in the ditches on the waterlogged sides of the highway.
I listened to the quiet narrow as we entered the city.

I loved the language my grandparents spoke: saying nothing, holding both my hands. Was the
pines that set off sound in them. My grandmother stared out the windshield and into the hills,
saying *That man, That man*. My grandfather shifted in his seat at the wheel, practicing owning
something. I had a feeling that I was the last let into the kingdom of their distance. Something
was owed, neither side would spell it out. I counted the fallen pines as the car dipped through
the hills in the tidewater, lonely as a dog with the whole world inside. I counted the pines and
put my voice inside them.

BOLAÑO BLUED

The forest is bordered by the highway to the west and the railroad tracks to the east;
here, like a dead man, I never sleep. I'm the moon, soon the sea, darkening in apology.

My sickness is antithetical— my accomplice or attempt: pride, rage, violence.
For a long time I wondered what English meant, if it was worth its weight in enlightenment:

everything slow and asthmatic; everything disgustingly still, frozen somewhere
in the air. Maybe that's why I can't express want I what— two words strung together;

maybe that's why I lived alone and did nothing for three years. Loneliness is an aspect
of human authorization, verbal egotism. I write to understand stillness, not to praise.

To name is to please, to keep awake: all please to the highway—
swells, bursts. I'm going to show a film now I'm going to show a film

now: yesterday, to keep awake, I dreamed I lived inside the agitation of silence, a hollow
building in Barcelona, the abandoned Mediterranean (blue), a tree turning the lights on and off.

Occasionally it shook, the monkey applauding in the corner. Fade to black. Everything gleams
like the wind in the rocks. The sad stories I must tell you, the gesture that never came,

the trigger pulled at the worst possible moment.
Audience.

CONSIDER THE DEER

Consider the deer who, when I say *deer*, doesn't know
whether or not I mean a single one, though there were two
dead and shiny with maggots on the side of the highway;
or, a group of them, always a bit lost
in the divided woods (blame our need to reach
or leave each other, faster).

Consider the deer that I saw dead
on the shoulder, midday mid-autumn,
whose neck in post-rigor-mortis pining
broke itself again so that the head could face
the woods, the woods setting itself alight.
Oh, that I could turn and live again, the deer might say,
recalling that one poet singing to himself, ruining the grass.

Consider that the deer, when called, won't come alone
purely due to linguistic vagary. Who, like me, resists
the gesture toward singularity.
Call my name and the whole woods
rise up inside me. I is a plural state
of being. Consider the multitude
before my footfall; how I'm able to crane my neck back,
see only myself.

THIS SIGN IS AVAILABLE

Tell me if I'm coming on too strong: I don't think my anti-capitalism phase is a phase Perhaps

gender is my greatest product No, I'd like to be as animal as language Poems are bullshit unless

they're acres of land Would you believe oil money pays for my poems? I'm talking a lot

these days, saying phrases like agrarian societies hoping you'll get the hint When was the last time

you listened to your fruit? What I fear most, since we're being honest, isn't that human ingenuity

will set the earth on fire, but that we won't know we started it Every day I take up space

on the internet, I'm sure someone has died for that comfort I was going to lie to you about how much

I enjoyed shooting a gun If I was a billboard, I'd play a continuous loop of a video appropriately titled

"Buck Fever" in which a young girl trembles with joy after killing her first buck

Sometimes language is the animal, sometimes it's the gun In one myth, my grandfather was

the biggest pimp the city had seen What does family mean then? Who's your daddy?

SELF/HOOD

Wearing today the diacritical preconception of otherness

Approached thusly and code-ified, solidified in speech

Wrongness worn and singled out signaling

The palimpsest: I

I wrung and wrought at the intersection

I against the map, axes of which lack my name

Made in whose image, whose mirror do I refuse?

Autoerotic automata: in one scene the self is what I wear

To travel the rivulet of touching

Sensing myself, how do I return?

No name in the city of undoing

I lengthen beyond what I know

ECCLESIASTES

How to testify? In the marketplace
for my voice was everything was meaningless.
Knee-deep in the mud with my tongue out.
monsoon. mason jar. morning glory.
Must I carry even the idiolect of gravel;
glossolalia and stupor of all things
moving and unmoving?

I fall in and fall back out.

Oh, exaltation! the Virginia pine grows
straight up to deeper blue,
and most taproots I'll never see.
I was waiting for you to turn around
pretending none of this baffles me.
Not taking it personally.

GO-GO ODE

O capacious room,
give me your tongues.

I'm done with being self-
possessed. Take hold, turn

the river in me. I'm freed
up to be anybody else,

my molecules twinned
with the sound. O erotic ours,

pass me not. Keep me in
the pocket. O percussive

dissent, devotion is anything you say
go awry. In this early hour,

keep me recursive. The impulse is
to lose my feet. I'm yet overcome.

You seismic drop.
You sovereign fade.

O black chaos, I'm in study
at your center, turn me out.

[NEW IMPRESSIONZ FOUND MYSELF A CLAPPA]

Though I'm practical and would rather watch
the room fill and fold like a black sea
turning over, I'll be your disciple.

I'll follow where you pull me, which, you
walking before me, makes me forget
my creditors. Pressing up on me in the houseparty,

pressing on me so that I could be the wall
holding up the house with my desire. Violent pleasure
I welcome, your weight. You asked me into study,

pressing up like that. I work for your weight
against me. I was saying something like   {I don't care about commerce}
when you kept asking that narrow question

about my body. Baby, I'm undoing myself behind you.
You, shaken down to what the drums give, and
I found myself, found myself inside this

homeless groove you can't name. Can't name me except being
given over to the usness we make for the next 90 seconds.

Sometimes I feel so outside. Then you invite me in.
This is how I keep time, and I keep to it, you inviting me in.

[ABM CAN'T FEEL MY FACE]

Running into you on U street one spring night puts a texture to my economic anxiety and social grief. Running back the macrofeel in the monastic field of thought, riding the black morning bus to the wealthtrap. What did you think of the housecleaners and the au pairs and the people working the land bused in with us? I had a feeling to ask, judging by the electric motherfucker sadness that was in the educational zoo within a school we were shown in. Which is to say, I could feel you then. Some bootstrap theory we were given over to and resounded in. The music of a quarter in your pocket when I need it was all I needed to continue; *money ain't a thing* but the holes in my timbs. *I can't feel my face* because you were acting it out and I loved you for that. I wondered who I was realizing I was just like you.

MAGNITUDE AND BOND

We were, all of us, ethered
       when the window broke. Soon after, the floor
           bent. The wood collapsing upon

itself formed a new dimension,
       a new danger. I wanted to kiss
           all of you, friends— on the scruff, in the DJ booth,
              behind the table in the blue screenlight

I played what you wanted. In the middle of our going on,
       jealousy was the snow thawing on a good day: obfuscation, then
           bright destruction. My desire in the cold months was

opaque, egalitarian. We were driven and making it up
       hip to hip. No matter the rhythm the beat
           laid out, salt on our lips:

our primary concern, our formal plea. Amber-lit
       halfway by the sodium light, we wanted darkness
           only, save for blunts, save for someone lighting

a cigarette. Desire is a blue dimension.
       I played you collapsing, bent by
           need to the floor.

CLUB 2718

Because I don't have the juice or enough gold anything to enter, a room that occasionally exists inside of me is the poorly lit dance floor of Club 2718. Thirst is a way of knowing, not knowing. I was on a gin-fueled hunt for big asses and music I could cry to. A woman almost twice my age asks where I've been and she shuts the door. Like any american what haunts me is my addiction to private property, not time or blackness. I want to love no one in particular the way I say I love my woman when she's in the doorway and mad at me. There were days I believed my grandfather owned my grandmother, kept her overfed and out of the sun in the back room. Occasionally a room exists inside of me where Johnny Hartman & John Coltrane's "My One and Only Love" plays on repeat. On repeat too is a video of my grandfather dancing a limber-legged shuffle and singing across the wall to my grandmother. To love like him is to be a student of regret. To abide by regret is to watch grief turn to ecstasy. I wept in the winter when I left my woman, I wept in the heat when she came back.

A KIND OF WILDNESS DESCENDS AND ACROSS THE EXPANSE THE ATTENDANT WIND DRONES ITS ONE FECUND SONG

When I am so tender in the thick
of rot I let all the morning wet

spread a plague across this threadbare
vessel that holds in what hums, what rushes beneath.

give as the ground gives:

Make of me your groveling tongue your dust.
Your   possessed   possessing.

never let up.

ON IGNORANCE

O fear fulcrum, desire is that plant we can't name.

What can I say?

I felt like rubbing my anthers
all over your exposed legs.

If I turn to you
I turn to kindling.

O furry trouble, nigh
behind me as I pace the woods.

O hearth in the clearing,
look at what I break
into to look away—

AUBADE

There is much to do. The room is red
because we are indecent. The light gives me up.
I've made myself at home: I sit on your porch,
watch— the light leads the field past the dumpsters
amber to green; all the wasps huddle in the weaker part
of the rocking chair; briefly, I see my breath then I don't.

I talk to my other lover on the phone about the certain sounds
some birds make down here this early, not their particular music
but their surety, how they seem to know only one song
and to sing it to its bleating end:

O, to call your name only, to be that sure.

Like the light I am scattered
I've come to need dispersal. It's morning again and
I know nothing about you— your arm is sweaty,
heavy across my chest.

W 177TH & BROADWAY

All night you eyed the man I wanted to be;
my jaw flexed tight. Anger slipped into
desire. Easily he would rise. Easily you would
disperse, pleasure made into light:
what you want under him,
I put on to amuse— I, your worked
supplicant. Yes, love is looking away.
My desire greened in your dismissal. Was
technicolor and twilight-made and never
turning off. The city air hung humid
above our charade. What need I could fill:
to transubstantiate, to unravel?

THIS IS A REVIEW FOR BLUE IN GREEN BY MILES DAVIS

It's raining. Has to be raining. Someone in the corner room is in love with you. Loves you enough to touch her body, wants you to watch; pull up a chair. The horn asks: *How long has it been since?* There are a number of feelings you are in need of. You are not sadness, but near. Down one road in your mind you are walking alone; down another everyone is your wife. The horn asks: *temperance, obedience*. In the corner room, the daybed pressed to spark against the wall, she came. When you leaned in to know about it, you wished she would've slapped your hand away; wished to unhear your name falling out of her.

BROOKLYN POEM

Love on the bridge. I can't stop singing about
how clean you broke me. Deny me again,

love on the fire escape saying *nevermind*,
nevermind, speaking low. If all this ends,

let me say now that in my solitude I pace
around the winter you pressed me up

against my kitchen wall. You were an appeal
to my loneliness, not its end. We

swallowed the white light,
chanted the same lament down.

Love on the light bus love holding my hand
up Fulton, love giving me your cheek,

letting my hand slip. I thought you came here
with some music some tending to.

I wanted to burn money with you, or for you.
No matter baby, immateriality is

our ontological birthright. A hard cider,
the light in my hands, then   levitation.

METAPHYSICS

In your simple palace,

I let my lamp lithe emit

light. O shipmate,

our atlas is a chasm

of ache. Come as steam

to the slip. Touch is the myth-

path we pattern and latch.

Patch the split mile,

O ayah of calm.

For you, I take off my pelt.

I melt.

ART MOVIE

Red is a secret in the trees. The train passes through the trees in Alabama. Red earth red earth. The winterlight consumes the field. The light silvers. The light relieves. The light thrown as dust upon the field I put my ear in. I crack an egg, and a saxophone that tells on me, yells at me, comes out no yolk. The train hollers to stop. The train stopped, still loads new passengers, but the conductor won't let me get off and kiss you. You know that's what I haunted to do. The stage is the window circle between us. The emergency exit door. I keep you in my ear and give you how I'm doing and what I want to eat were I not on a train. You and your white boots. You tell me what else could come out of an egg— women all the way down, holding waists. The train is a place going by, strictly passing through. I touch a stranger's wrist going back to my seat, the whole train becomes a garment I put on. I touch indiscriminately. I can't stay, I tell the dog waving from your convertible. None of the windows open. I held your gaze until I couldn't. In the previous scene, I took you to the slip until we were shining tunnels for sound. I took your sound for my name. Never asked what I called myself.

I SET OUT TO TOUCH IT ALL OVER

Justin Phillip Reed

The way the field expands is a terror is
the liminal space we speak of when we speak on
the going between. I'm saying it the same again: nothing
here is tethered to nothing else where the here is
the body, mine. Yet everything incongruous: the robins
tear the worms from their dirtbeds, when it rains,
the worms again tarry in the dirt. Do and get done to.
I come to seek to come to it. It being the
bodymine, the walk through
to listening. I listened to mine, the body, the field,
and still this hole.

MY IDEA OF ABSTRACTION IS WHITE LIGHTNING

Jack Whitten

Halfway between Gonyon and Ophelia   imminent splendor.   It doesn't matter what I don't know.

Clouds creating a blue fissure in the sky,   whose grammar   whose sadness hurries forth?

I want to speak to order: soybeans, corn, wheat rows browned to torpor.

Mercy.   Protozoan, water-shorn,   hotly I listen   in the pines for my green name.   Whoever can

stop reasoning, stop.   Is it too much to ask   to be remade   I who've just begun?

Adagio of light, copper-hued diadem

hanging on twilight's hem, Virginia sun— I'm yet released from the

sharp language of being: make me another by morning   lest I stay

in this vestibule   wholly unmade.

TRANS IS AGAINST NOSTALGIA

Every day I build the little boat,
my body boat, hold for the unique one,
the formless soul, the blue fire
that coaxes my being into being.

Yes, there was music in the woods, and
I was in love with the trees, and a beautiful man
grew my heartbeat in his hands, and there
was my mother's regret that I slept with.

To live there is pointless. I'm building the boat,
the same way I'd build a new love—
looking ahead at the terrain. And the water
is rising, and the generous ones are moving on.

O New Day, I get to build the boat!
I tell myself to live again.
Somehow I made it out of being 15
and wanting to jump off the roof

of my attic room. Somehow I survived
my loneliness and throwing up in a jail cell.
O New Day, I've broken my own heart. The boat
is still here, is fortified in my brokeness.

I've picked up the hammer every day
and forgiven myself. There is a new
language I'm learning by speaking it.
I'm a blind cartographer, I know the way

fearing the distance. O New Day,
there isn't a part of you I don't love
to fear. I'm holding hands with
the poet speaking of light, saying *I made it up*

I made it up.

SEMIOTICS

In the dream, I am my father riding through
the Thai countryside with a banjo playing itself
in the passenger seat. Strapped in like a baby.

The light fallen so thick it makes a brass bowl
of the valley. The light articulating green
to the day. I want to sing it real, what I saw

with his eyes. Like a river sings
to an ocean, until the river is a cloud.
Sing the song a cloud sings to

a mountain. Sing it true, and liquid the light.
The light fallen. I resonate. I green. I steam-ring
and undo my face. I let the new light undo my face:

I become my father's distance in the temple, the glinting
Buddha head casting gold between the floor and
his frayed shadow. His fallow voice repeats

the mantra *leave leave leave*, as he passes
glass beads between his fingers. My father
rocks side to side in prayer, I become that groove.

I weep as my father in devotion and anger.
We write the same letter to my mother:
you are you did youyouyouyou.

I become my father as speed on a highway,
the tape deck playing associations:
Father is to Fathomed as Phantom is to what?

The answers draw a sentence across the windshield
as crude lines. I'm a banjo driving, trying to read
the blueprint my father left. I think it was his voice.

LORDE BLUE

My deepest and rational non-knowledge fears this depth too much
to examine it. A well of replenishing force, approximate
attempt is enough. Fully I can feel in the doing, the doing for

which I rise up, (even at its most difficult?), requires a question not only of what
but how I enter, root and satisfaction, gratefully; fullness is closer. Or
oblivion— I move toward/through the self: discipline, abnegation,

erotics of the ascetic: my body opens into response, opens to building an idea:
my capacity to demand from all knowledge an afterlife.
Raised to yes, my cravings, obedient, live outside myself. And yes,

there is a looking away, a travesty of necessity— call it something else: a fit.
In the satisfying, I have a particular feeling, male
was not available when I was trying this sensation.

CONJECTURE ON THE NATURE OF INCONVENIENCE

If I pull the hanged man's card on new year's eve, then I am telling on myself.

If the body is said to be either   or   , then I am telling on myself.

If the body is said to be either   or   , then there is a liminality unaccounted for.

If there is an unaccounted liminality, then there is a dispossession.

If there is a body dispossessed, then there is a hole in the language.

If there is a hole in the language, then I am slipping through, stealing away.

If I am slipping, then I'm not on my way anywhere.

If I'm not on my way anywhere, then I can be a kind of futility.

If I am futile, then I am a fugitive against the idea of linear movement.

If I am against movement, then I am against passing for.

If I am passing, then I am a boy.

If I am a boy, then I am holding something stolen.

If I'm assumed to be holding something stolen, then I am in an elevator in new york.

If I'm in an elevator in new york, then I am about to look down the throat of a gun.

If the gun doesn't speak, then I'm ~~still here~~ lucky.

If I'm lucky, then she wasn't crying when she called the cops on me.

If the neighbor called the cops on me, then I never saw her that morning.

If she never saw me, then I am a theory of myself.

If I am an unsubstantiated claim, then I am a figment of her anxiety.

If I am a figment, then my death would be inconsequential.

If I didn't die, then she will send me flowers apologizing for her inconvenience.

If I was already an inconvenience to the language, then she is right.

If she is right, then there is an elsewhere to which I belong.

If there is an elsewhere, then there is a clearing in the woods.

If there are woods, then there is a ground that abstains ruin.

If there is a ground, then there are bodies beneath it.

If the bodies know my name, then I am said to be protected.

If I am spoken for, then I could've died a number of times.

If I am still here, then I am speaking for the dirt.

If there is dirt, then there is my mouth wet and ripe with questions.

FROM THE NEVER

Clarice Lispector

To notice with the whole body
the body's imprecision to want
to exceed the body,
to flee. Is to come from
the never to hold all
the embers in the mouth
and not once smoke out
the body's exits?
I lied my way into this
body of egregious error
good abhorrent body
needed adored body
feed on me please body
more or less easy body
unfinished almost
body and its dirt pact
its sullied is mine,
mine.

CHIAROSCURO

Whereas I come into the into to talk with my shadow.
From you I've not hid my face.

For in the morning I make, and am made by you:
beautiful projection, boy in the mirror, boy in my mind.
I separate my flesh from my flesh to become more
like you, to drown in your holdings.

O young lord of my desire, you are the light
I ride toward, I run from. I eat less and avoid
being hailed. Anonymous interstitial prince
of my undoing, redeemer of my yes, I want

to grow into you, and then abandon your
imprecise naming. I am bequeathed violence—
your inheritance— and your rough glamour.

I am made to tarry, here, with you,
thus illumined by your tenuous light.

VIRGINIA SLIM

                                                    velvet

                                                    myth

muscadines   at twilight.

                                        our imagination

                                        caught a rabbit

                                    . I lit his cigar

                                    — I stuffed my mouth

                                    landless

                                        I rode

by lamplight   to the edge of

                        his house,   what are you supposed to believe;

green hope   am I   to enter the world

                                                    low: in the dirt:

bit,

black

THE OLD HOUSE, FOR THOSE WHO KNOW HOW TO LISTEN, IS A SORT OF GEOMETRY OF ECHOES. // GASTON BACHELARD // THE POETICS OF SPACE

THE BLACK PROLETARIANIZATION OF THE BOURGEOIS FORM ISN'T KANYE WEST'S GOSPEL SAMPLES

O, Death. Your singular eye. My mother speaks the King's English. Makes quiche. Makes clove pomanders in winter. Pawned her flute. Cleaned my elementary school classroom. What is hers? Brillant song, my mother, sotto voce, in her chair asking for touch. It is drowning she means, not freedom. I swam fine. Don't you get it, O Death, my mother is elegant alive, entering the blue hole of evening, alone. You could reach into the frame, pull her out. O Death, I've been crueler— I've watched.

BLACK EXISTENTIAL EXEGESIS

This engine and cog business is wigged out. I want nothing we're owed from the ship gig, thence, the land whereon modern sound weaned off our cowrie and cached aged conjure. Land whereon our woe is chic and wanted. Shoutout to every nigga cajoled into winging it in a crowd, crowing about being the hewer and the hewer's subject. O my aching chore choir, dew upon our ochre echo throughout this land, this cadence gag. Our eco-ego greeded upon and caged. Grace is our awed crowd which encores green and geodes. Shoutout to every nigga dodging age by ignoring human genre fiction gore. Ergo, we're nowhere reneging on being owned, and renewed weighing nothing like race. Shoutout to every nigga eroding off the edge of something else gossamering the air.

8TH & INGRAHAM

I forget about money watching the clouds over 8th & Ingraham. The clouds a rhubarb-colored ship in the sky. To my right it all grays out, the bats emerging now from the chimneys. The bats listening for the cicadas' echo. Echo is a way to create space, is a metaphor for time. Time for the cop to move along I think watching the cop watch me from my porch. Fuck 12. The robin on the wirevine the wireeye competing with the bats for cicadas. The robin competing reds with the sky. The sky a money for the cicadas: a way to make space, time. The cicadas sounding out the future through repetition. A friend says to spend nothing is to keep flexibility in your hands, to keep your youth. Money the sound of decay. Money the repetition of waste.

JUNE, DC

It hit 95° at the brightest part of the day. Today, Sue asked me if I was an artist outside the poems. I made a Bachelard joke about drawing imaginary lines and forgot to answer her question. They raised the metro fare again. Parts of the red line are down for six months. Thank god the train makes me anxious. Ever since spotting the plainclothes. It stays light late and I've got the porch fan on, so maybe I'll be outside until tomorrow. I'm not in love with anyone. Since I've been on the porch reading O'Hara say the names of his dead pals, one jumpout car rolled by stacked too tight with four 12, slow rolling in their tan sedan. It's hot out. The last shooting was in April on 6th and Longfellow. There's a tree in front of my house that needs to be cut down. I'm the one to do it. The bark is going white and peeling off. There's gray spores coating the leaves. Hummingbirds are meant for summer, they swim in the air. The honeysuckle bush will start to sing at twilight. I can't watch the blue jays anymore, there goes my grandfather. Wholetime there's been a mourning dove on the wirevine. I told my friend in Providence that I've been attuned to all these human privacies. Like what just happened: a man gave his friend a round of applause when he got into the car. As if I'd been given, in this season, new eyes. I'm not in love with anyone, but what else can I call the way I buried my face in the purple salvia plant in the bouquet I got from the farm share. Everything unfolds magnificent around me. Somehow, a few miles away, men with high cholesterol and no respect for language want to sell my life back to me. Or take me out. I get ten credit card offers a week. It's 95° and no weather for a binder, I say to the dying tree, the mourning dove, the wirevine carrying my secrets. I walk down Kennedy and think of my grandmother who I didn't know I could love. How I wept in the hospice room, kissed by her swollen tongue. Summers are for lovers and a quiet death in the house. A new friend asked me where my wildness lives, and I remembered that I have a body. The clovers have taken over the front yard. I'm not in love, and so have no one to whisper this to.

HUNGER

Dear Justin,

No meals this week, but a new poem almost everyday. I am concerned by my hunger, as much as I am inured to it. Addicted to emptiness maybe. The mystics didn't eat and were thus transformed, and transcended the flesh. Is anyone a mystic these days? Seeing past the body-artifice and looking back at the panopticon? Are you drinking water where you are? DC put out a boil advisory for 72 hours because a sewage pipe broke and contaminated the water. Those kinds of mistakes are never mistakes. I might walk to a friend's house and use her faucet. I'm walking everywhere and I'm thirsty and not fucking. Thankfully, my one pair of shoes held out this year. Found some dried black beans and rice in the cabinet: grace! I wish our intellect could materialize into food. I want to cook us a full meal. Maybe one day when we're up next in the rotation of wealth, we'll trade sous vide recipes, and I'll perfect exotic fruit pies, and we'll eat seafood and we'll have clean water. I'm feeling like the wind, touching everything when I'm walking through the city. I'm so light, I'm only light. Started smoking my emergency stash of cigarettes. Working on making those last, cutting them with weed. So many new thoughts in my hunger, I'm staying in the woods longer and learning self-reliance from the trees. Did you eat today? Who am I except my discipline, I say to myself when I've got choices.

SELF-PORTRAIT IN CYANOTYPE

The blue interval beckons, threatens
to spill into my rough form. My long face.
What is this distance from myself? I own
some amateur, liminal fade.
No substance. All ether. Being
dithers like sound under water.
The dark is blue as the light.
All solid is else, vanishing.
This blue lust. This lessness
between selves. I'll abide
the weather and blur.

STATES OF DECLINE

The room is dying honey and lemon rind.
Soured light. My grandmother sits in her chair

sweetening into the blue velvet. Domestic
declension is the window that never opens—

the paint peeling, dusting the sill, and inhaled.
It is an american love she lives in,

my grandmother, rigored to televangelists
and infomercials. Losing the use of her legs.

Needing to be turned like a mattress.
No one is coming for her. The dog is

asleep in the yard, her husband,
obedient to the grease and garlic

in the cast iron, salting her
death in the wind house.

RIGOROUS PRACTICE OF LISTENING

By which I mean we let the day pass between us
without either of us saying *go on* or *stay*, saying much of anything.
That when you did speak it was in the language of birds— your hands raised
as wings to your mouth blowing in and out,
the birds came from their high places amongst the pines,
singing back to you.

There was the man who you said nothing to but kissed his forehead
after he'd caught us three fish. And the man who fixed your cars
who never spoke. The stranger you shared a cigar with in front of the grocery store.
The way you held the package of red beans from your brother back home. I heard it all.

Who knows how your brilliant uncles died
or how many people you saw given over to trees
or left on the train tracks.
When I ask you about fear, you take me to the nectarine tree
where the beetles have eaten halfway through.
I can't kill them, you say, *but they'll destroy the whole yard*.

VIRGINIA SLIM

Young buck tapping
its velvet against the
bathroom window in
the morning. The land
leaning in the pines,
the well, cattails,
muscadines, hot metal
in the shed, chicory on
the stove at twilight. In
the orange morning I
rose w/ my grandfather,
w/ the larger animals
of our imagination, and
warmed the truck to go
to the water. On the
way I laid down in the
truck bed and caught a
rabbit barely in the
grasp of a hawk. What
did I know about being
hunted? I knew
everything. The meek
don't inherit shit— I
stuffed my mouth with
pine needles and spit, bled
and spit, at the
root, and look where it's
got me— landless. If
the water was a myth, then

I went in looking
for my dog only to find
my grandmother's
armchair. I rode it as I
would any wet story—
to deeper blue. Listen:
by lamplight my
grandfather would lead
me to the edge of the
woods—*this is yours*—
then he would kill the
light. If I told you he
flew back to his house,
what are you supposed
to believe; it was just
me and my green hope
pressing through the
black. How else am I
supposed to enter the
world if I'd already left
once: as myth: not set
apart: but as a small
shelled thing: low:
toiling in the dirt: lifting
every bit of black to
breathe

CONTAINING CONTINUITY

How to talk about wonder about the horn (I'm listening to Christian Scott) without saying horn or trumpet, and resisting abstraction. The furthest I can get is that the sound comes from the corner, is continually, in motion and resisting form, a kind of stasis or staticness. The sound is a hovering. A presence pressure. Sound wraith. Wraith's whir. The sound is in response and also asks a question, or a few. To say I'd fallen into failure, or failure had illuminated itself in front of me, is one truth. I am a victim of light, but what else is new.

In Finland, I hear John Coltrane say *I'm sorry, they thought I was* and *...without me I was starting without me*. What vacillates between precision and error? practicepracticepractice. I stood up when I heard his voice. Sound isn't the problem, my problem, it's the translation that's tripping me and catching me in a trance, the need to translate one abstraction into another. What am I saying and to whom. Thought moves my hand to gesture, to make letter bodies that sound together, which create some kind of assumption by association. It's true, in a field I can experience the largess of language. One song says spread out, one songs says small up yourself. Is this a poem yet? In a field my thoughts are at home in uncertainty. The wind plays the horn in the corner, the grass is an insistence a snare repeat. See, there's instruments, names in the way.

I want a series of *mhmms* in the language to hold over ecstaticism. The various portmanteaus of my home could do: *wylin* (wild and wily, maybe some assertion of will) to mean out of place and beyond. To approximate to horn's appearance I can say: *that joint go*— meaning a continuation, a lack of arrival or departure, a way out through around. That the horn resists audience, it just go. And where are we going getting somewhere?

What I seek when I seek to talk to you about what the sounds do to me is to convey a kind of dynamism. I was avoiding another task, perhaps writing, when I first heard Christian Scott, then I could only write, and if I wasn't writing I was pacing the apartment, making lines with my body. If you were here, I'd pass you the j. Something is to be said about where the sounds take me; that I'm in my house pacing is one reality. That the horn sends me to an elsewhere, another. *Darling you Darling you honest you do*, Sam Cooke might say *send me*, that's one line I draw. To be sweet on the sound. An ethereal knowing and meaning-making I'm trying to get across. I listened to Christian Scott into the night and tried to become sound. See what I mean? There's a gap. Perhaps it's fear. The sound was a kind of devastation across my body such that I was changed and seek out that feeling, continually, such that I need to tell you about it.

May I be made into the vessel of that which / must be made, Bidart says, and I think of hot metal dissolving into sound, or further back the first human moan that turned a corner into singing, entered another room in the mind.

What gender should I be in this sound? I want you to ask you who are still here, when I hear some trap music some shit I never heard? and in the corner two women dancing on each other almost identically dressed, whining one's ass up on the other. I don't want to be either of them, I want to be what's between them. Impossible desire in ecstatic physicality. Heat made tangible. Yes opening to yes. When my woman puts her ass on me, my feelings are hurt. I'm wrecked. I'm her tool. I'm a tower of light. An ancient loss of control. Impossible desire. What sound is that?

DERRIDA/COLEMAN

Were it possible, I would be naked. Of the nude philosophy:
consider the globalization of the expensive american sound.

Should we worry? We should work. I believe you're right.
I distrust the word "white." It's sanctified propaganda.

Repetition is my language of origin, the highest technology. Anyway
the body is only mine provisionally. For reasons that I'm not sure of,
I am convinced that before becoming music, music was only a word.

I prefer to destroy the composer, renew the concept.
Extraordinary limitation playing freedom.

SIMILES

Nothing is *like* jail. Nothing resembles it or approximates it. Nothing is *like* being detained, except for being detained. Nothing is slower than time then. Time is measured between who you were before being handcuffed and who you'll be stumbling out the jail onto the small-town street with no one to talk to. Who you'll be is measuring each breath that isn't metallic air. How is the air after the bruise on your rib? It's nothing like air. Nothing is like being alone when you shouldn't be alone. Alone is the fear of being watched and not speaking for weeks. Nothing is like a cage but a cage, I tell this to myself. Knowing where I've been. Knowing where I have to go.

ON MY WAY TO YOU

Everyday is an invitation into intimacy, I decide, leaving my house.

That I would cross it, given the distance. Being money myself

and having none in the form of new shoes and all these holes in my jacket.

I inherited this privacy, given what it's like to be an instrument—

Given each plant singing in its season. Given the trees between.

How can I tell you, given that you abide, I zeroed out in the field.

Given the no place of the soul. Given the soul ringing in the forest's

hollows. Given to ringing, being money myself given away.

Given the language this image system produces. Given that distance.

Given how maroon the morning war sky I wake up in,

owning nothing being money myself. Given that the block is mine

sayeth the red-eyed gods slouched over, standing up in exquisite coats.

Given trouble and home in the city that slipped out one night.

Given Uptown, Trinidad, KDY, wolves in Rock Creek. Given to corn-syrup spilling

out the cornerstore. Given the technicolor hole of the cornerstore. Given 7th & Florida,

that chromophonic praise break at the intersection. Given that happenstance touch.

Given the distance of money, I'm from nowhere where I'm from.

Being not monied myself and given to language. Given and being let go.

That distance. That I could cross it, given that you can hear me.

ACKNOWLEDGMENTS

Grateful acknowledgment is made to the editors of these journals where some of the poems appeared: *Revolute*, *Mumber Magazine*, *Scalawag*, *Academy of American Poets*, *The Offing*, *The Rumpus*, *The Paris Review*, *The Baffler*, *Four Way Review*, *HEArt Online*, *spacecraftproject*, *Indiana Review*, *BOAAT*, *Tin House*, *Iron Horse Literary Review*, *The Shade Journal*, *Vinyl Poetry & Prose*, *wildness*, *Callaloo*, and *Split This Rock*.

Light upon light to my line, my teachers, and those who've loved and thought with me. This book is dedicated to my first teacher David Elijah Hayes Sr. This book is dedicated to everyone I've passed walking in DC, all the strangers who've engaged me in conversation, those who've listened next to me, who I might never meet again.

Light upon light to you whom I'm in continual study with: fahima ife, Nabila Lovelace, Justin Phillip Reed, Jonah Mixon-Webster, Jayson P. Smith, S*an D. Henry-Smith, Camonghne Felix, Sarah Barnes, Xandria Phillips, Chekwube Danladi, Jenny Xie, Marwa Helal, and Elizabeth Bryant. Thank you to Phillip B. Williams and Dante Micheaux who saw the earliest versions of this book and believed in it.

To Laini Mataka, Vievee Francis, Greg Pardlo, Molly Chehak, Monica Youn, Natalie Diaz, and Ross Gay, thank you for the generosity of your instruction, for your listening. Thank you to the fellows, faculty, and staff of the Cave Canem retreats in 2016, 2017, and 2019; the fellows of the 2015 Callaloo Workshop; and the 2017 Conversation Literary Festival fellows.

This book is made possible through the love and brilliance of my people: Marie Tattiana Aqeel, Be Steadwell, Saa Joy, Kailasa Aqeel, David Roswell, Maggie Heraty, Brenda Hayes, Caitlin O'Neill, Chinwe Okona, Asher Kolieboi, Warren Harding, Tiesha Cassel, Afia Ofori-Mensa, Pep Felton, the whole Steadwell-Swearingen crew.

Light upon light to Fred Moten for sitting with me and some comrades into the night in Oberlin in 2013. That conversation set me on my path, thank you.

Thank you to everyone who fed me and listened to me during my time in Paris. Particular shoutout to the ghost of Ted Joans.

Light upon light to Carey Salerno and everyone at Alice James Books who participated in making this book a reality.

Thank you, reader, for sitting with me.

Light upon light to the trees that made this exchange possible.

RECENT TITLES FROM ALICE JAMES BOOKS

Alice James Books is committed to publishing books that matter. The press was founded in 1973 in Boston, Massachusetts as a cooperative, wherein authors performed the day-to-day undertakings of the press. This element remains present today, as authors who publish with the press are invited to collaborate closely in the publication process of their work. AJB remains committed to its founders' original feminist mission, while expanding upon the scope to include all voices and poets who might otherwise go unheard. In keeping with its efforts to build equity and increase inclusivity in publishing and the literary arts, AJB seeks out poets whose writing possesses the range, depth, and ability to cultivate empathy in our world and to dynamically push against silence. The press was named for Alice James, sister to William and Henry, whose extraordinary gift for writing went unrecognized during her lifetime.

Designed by Tiani Kennedy

Printed by McNaughton & Gunn